A Kid's Guide to Drawing America™

How to Draw
Louisiana's
Sights and Symbols

Jenny Deinard

The Rosen Publishing Group's
PowerKids Press™
New York

Published in 2002 by The Rosen Publishing Group, Inc.
29 East 21st Street, New York, NY 10010

First Edition

Book Design: Kim Sonsky
Layout Design: Michael Donnellan
Project Editor: Jennifer Landau

Illustration Credits: Jamie Grecco except p. 27 by Emily Muschinske.
Photo Credits: p. 7 © Philip Gould/CORBIS; pp. 8, 9 © Morris Museum of Art, Augusta, Georgia; pp. 12, 14 © One Mile Up, Incorporated; p. 16 © Peter Smithers/CORBIS; pp. 18, 28 © Index Stock; p. 20 © W. Wayne Lockwood, M.D./CORBIS; p. 22 © Michael Freeman/CORBIS; p. 24 © Buddy Mays/CORBIS; p. 26 © Stephen Frink/CORBIS.

Deinard, Jenny
        How to draw Louisiana's sights and symbols /
Jenny Deinard.
        p. cm. — (A kid's guide to drawing America)
        Includes index.
        Summary: This book explains how to draw some of Louisiana's sights and symbols, including the state seal, the official flower, and St. Louis Cathedral in the French Quarter.
        ISBN 0-8239-6074-9
        1. Emblems, State—Louisiana—Juvenile literature 2. Louisiana—In art—Juvenile literature
3. Drawing—Technique—Juvenile literature [1. Emblems, State—Louisiana 2. Louisiana 3. Drawing—Technique]
        I. Title II. Series
        2001
        743'.8'99763—dc21

Manufactured in the United States of America

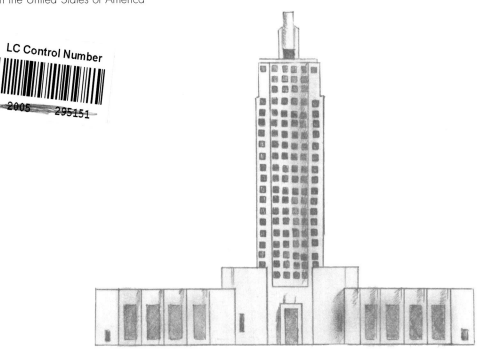

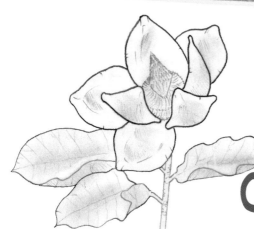

CONTENTS

Let's Draw Louisiana

In 1682, French explorer René-Robert Cavelier, known as La Salle, traveled to the region where the Mississippi River flows into the Gulf of Mexico. He named this area Louisiana, after King Louis XIV of France. French traditions still play an important role in Louisiana's culture. Many of Louisiana's residents are Cajun. They are descendants of the French Canadians who migrated from Nova Scotia, Canada, in the 1700s. Another group of Louisianans are Creole, people of French, Spanish, African, and Caribbean ancestry. In 1803, President Thomas Jefferson bought land from France that reached from the Mississippi River to the Rocky Mountains and from the Gulf of Mexico to Canada. This new territory, which became known as the Louisiana Purchase, doubled the size of the United States.

Long before the arrival of European explorers, Louisiana was home to several Native American groups, such as the Choctaw and the Caddo. The Kisatchie National Forest is named after the Caddo Native American word for "long cane."

In this book, you can learn more about Louisiana's exciting sights and symbols. You can learn how to draw them, too. The drawings start with simple shapes. You add other shapes to complete the drawing. Each new step is shown in red. The drawing terms below list some of the shapes and words that you will see throughout the book.

You will need the following supplies to draw Louisiana's sights and symbols:

- A sketch pad
- An eraser

- A number 2 pencil
- A pencil sharpener

These are some of the shapes and drawing terms you need to know to draw Louisiana's sights and symbols:

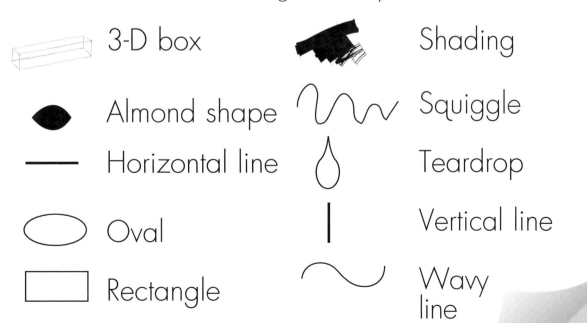

3-D box

Shading

Almond shape

Squiggle

Horizontal line

Teardrop

Oval

Vertical line

Rectangle

Wavy line

The Pelican State

Before the Civil War (1861–1865), Louisiana plantation owners, who grew cotton and sugar, were among the richest people in America. The war ended the plantation system, but since then Louisiana has become successful in other industries. When oil was discovered in 1901, Louisiana became a major producer of oil and natural gas. Louisiana became a state in 1812. It has a population of 4,372,000 and covers 49,651 square miles (128,596 sq km) of land. Baton Rouge, the capital city, has a population of 215,900.

Louisiana's official nickname is the Pelican State, because the eastern brown pelican is the state bird. It also is called the Bayou State because of its many lowland waterways, called bayous. Louisiana is perhaps best known for Mardi Gras. This two-month-long carnival is celebrated all around the state of Louisiana, but it is especially exciting in New Orleans.

During Mardi Gras, colorful floats, like the jester float shown here, head down St. Charles Avenue in New Orleans.

Louisiana Artist

Clementine Hunter

Clementine Hunter, the daughter of two former slaves in Louisiana, did not make her first painting until she was in her fifties. She couldn't sign her name to her paintings, because she could neither read nor write. Despite this Clementine Hunter became one of the most famous and gifted folk artists of her time. She created more than 4,000 paintings, many of which are hanging in galleries and in museums today. Hunter was born either in 1886 or 1887 on Hidden Hill Plantation, a cotton plantation near Cloutierville, Louisiana. At about the age of 15, she moved to the Melrose Plantation, where she spent the rest of her life. In 1938, Hunter met her friend Francois Mignon, who gave her the supplies for her first painting. Sometimes she even painted on old window shades. Over time Hunter's style became closely linked with a school of art known as outsider art. Outsider art, or folk art, is made by artists who have no formal training. Like many outsider artists' work, Hunter's paintings showed what she saw in her life, such as people working in the fields. Clementine Hunter died early in 1988, but she is remembered as one of this country's great folk artists.

Doing Laundry, painted by Hunter in 1963, is a good example of the strong shapes and bright colors used by outsider or folk artists. The images in folk painting are usually one-dimensional, which means that they appear flat on the canvas. This painting is done in oil on board and measures 16" x 23 ½" (41 cm x 60 cm).

Map of Louisiana

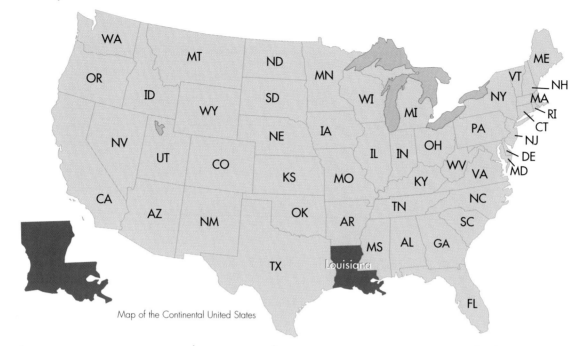

Map of the Continental United States

Louisiana is in the southeastern region of the United States and borders Mississippi, Arkansas, and Texas. Much of its border is formed by water, with the Mississippi River in the east, the Toledo Bend Reservoir in the west, and the Gulf of Mexico in the south. New Orleans is the lowest point in the state. Some areas of the city measure 8 feet (2 m) below sea level! The city lies between the Mississippi River and Lake Pontchartrain, which is a popular location for water sports. Levees built along the banks of the Mississippi River control flooding. The highest point in Louisiana is Driskill Mountain, in the northern part of the state, which measures 535 feet (163 m) above sea level.

1

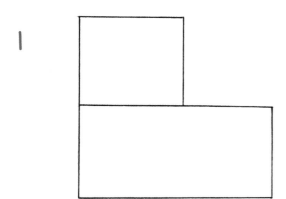

Start by drawing two rectangles.

2

Using the rectangles as a guide, draw the shape of Louisiana and the route of the Mississippi River. Erase any extra lines.

3

Draw in a circle to mark New Orleans.

4

Use a square to mark Port Hudson.

5

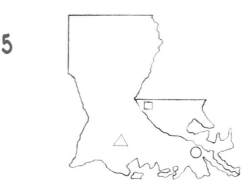

Use a triangle to mark Lake Fausse Pointe State Park.

6

Draw a star to mark Baton Rouge, the capital of Louisiana.

☆	Baton Rouge
	Mississippi River
○	New Orleans
□	Port Hudson
△	Lake Fausse Pointe State Park

7

To finish your map, draw a key in the upper right corner to mark the state's points of interest. Erase the extra lines in the star.

The State Seal

In 1902, William Wright Heard, who was Louisiana's governor at that time, selected the image that appears on the Louisiana state seal. The image shows a large eastern brown pelican, which is the state bird. The pelican has its head turned and is feeding three baby pelicans in their nest. Above the pelicans are the words "Union" and "Justice." Below the nest is the word "Confidence." Together these three words make up the state motto. The image is surrounded by the words "State of Louisiana."

1

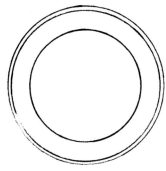

Start by drawing three large circles.

2

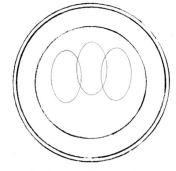

Add three ovals for the big pelican.

3

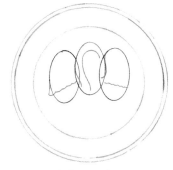

Draw the shape of the pelican using the ovals as a guide.

4

Erase extra lines and add four circles for the birds' heads.

5

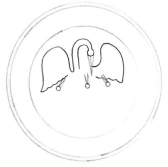

Add two triangles to each circle for the birds' beaks.

6

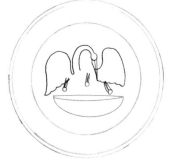

Draw in the nest using a half oval.

7

Add two stars and use ovals for the birds' bodies.

8

Finish the pelicans and write the words "STATE OF LOUISIANA ." In the small circle write "UNION, JUSTICE, CONFIDENCE." Erase extra lines and add detail.

13

The State Flag

Louisiana has had ten flags since Alonso de Pineda claimed the land for Spain in 1519. Throughout history Louisiana has been owned by Spain, France, and Great Britain. The United States bought it from the French in 1803. In 1810, American settlers turned Louisiana into an independent territory and created a new flag. This flag lasted until Louisiana became a state in 1812. During the Civil War, Louisiana flew the Confederate flag. Louisiana was readmitted to the Union in 1868, three years after the Civil War. In 1912, the present flag was adopted. The flag has a blue background with an image of a pelican feeding its young, the same as on the state seal.

1

Start by drawing a large rectangle for the flag's field.

2

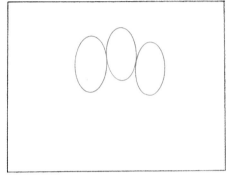

Add three ovals for the big pelican.

3

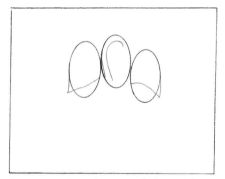

Begin drawing the shape of the pelican using the ovals as a guide.

4

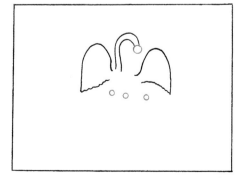

Erase extra lines. Add curved lines as shown. Add four circles for the four pelicans' heads.

5

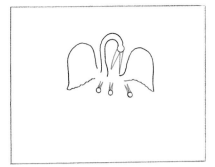

Add two triangles to each circle for the birds' beaks.

6

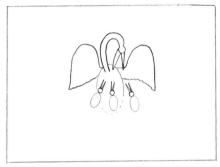

Then add a large oval for the big pelican and three small ovals for the baby pelicans.

7

Erase extra lines. Draw in the baby pelicans' bodies as shown. Add a half oval for the nest.

8

Add detail and shading and the words "UNION, JUSTICE & CONFIDENCE" to finish your flag.

15

The Magnolia Flower

Magnolia trees grow in many areas of Louisiana and around the world. You can find them in North America and Central America, in the Himalayan Mountains, in China, and in Japan. There are 80 different species of the magnolia, which was named after the seventeenth-century French botanist Pierre Magnol. Its blossom, the magnolia flower, was chosen as Louisiana's state flower on August 1, 1900. Magnolia flowers are large, fragrant, white flowers that are surrounded by thick, shiny leaves. They have from 6 to 12 petals. Some people use magnolia flowers as an herbal remedy to help relieve clogged nasal passages. The hard wood of the magnolia tree is used in furniture, cabinets, and doors.

1

Start by drawing a circle for the center of the flower.

2

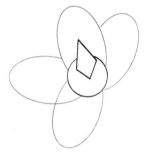

Add a diamond shape that reaches out from the center.

3

Erase the extra line and add four ovals for petals. The petals can overlap.

4

Add three triangles for petals. Use different sizes so the magnolia flower will look more natural.

5

Draw in the shape of the petals.

6

Erase extra lines.

7

Use a thin rectangle for the flower's stem, and three ovals for its leaves.

8

Add detail and shading. Erase any extra lines, and your flower is done.

The Bald Cypress

The bald cypress became Louisiana's official state tree in 1963. It grows in the swampy bayous, which make up more than 40 percent of the state's land. The bark on the bald cypress is reddish brown and fades to gray as the tree gets older. Round bumps, called knees, cover the wide trunk. They get their name because they look like human kneecaps. Bald cypress trees can grow from 50 to 70 feet (15–21 m) tall. They are hardwood trees and do not decay easily. This makes the bald cypress a good choice for building homes. Today many people in Louisiana live in century-old homes made from the wood of the bald cypress.

1

Start by drawing one large and one small triangle for the base of the tree.

2

Outline the tree and add two small rectangles for branches.

3

Erase extra lines. Redraw the bottom line of the tree trunk to make it wavy.

4

Draw the shape of the treetop using two ovals and two circles.

5

Add leaves around the circles and ovals using *V* shapes. Draw several lines on the bottom of the tree trunk.

6

Add shading and detail and you're done. You can also add extra branches and swamp water around the bald cypress tree.

The Eastern Brown Pelican

The eastern brown pelican became the state bird of Louisiana in 1966. Eastern brown pelicans are actually grayish brown with white markings on the tips of their feathers. Their heads are white and yellow, and they have long, flat bills, or mouths. To catch fish, eastern brown pelicans circle just above the water, dive under, and use their large throats to scoop up fish like a fisherman uses a net. They eat about 4 pounds (2 kg) of fish every day. In many areas, chemicals have polluted the waterways and have made it dangerous for the pelicans to eat fish. New laws protect the birds from these chemicals, and the population of eastern brown pelicans is growing.

1

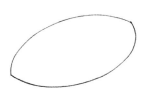

Start by drawing a large oval for the body.

2

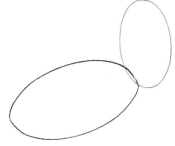

Add another oval for the neck shape.

3

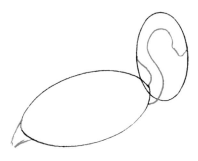

Draw in the shape of the pelican's neck and add tail feathers.

4

Erase extra lines.

5

Use two triangles to draw the pelican's beak and one triangle for the wing.

6

Draw in the pelican's wing and add two small rectangles for the legs. Draw in the pelican's beak pouch as shown.

7

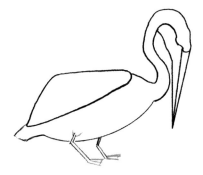

Erase extra lines and add small triangles for the bird's feet. Add detail to the leg.

8

Add an eye, some detail, and shading, and your bird is done.

The French Quarter

The French Quarter, a ten-block area along the Mississippi River, is one of the oldest sections of the city. It has historic buildings, shops, and cafés that serve good food and play jazz, blues, Dixieland, and Cajun music. Among the sights in the French Quarter is Jackson Square, a park that faces the beautiful St. Louis Cathedral. Other attractions include the Cabildo, which is the building where the Louisiana Purchase was signed, and the Old Butcher's Market, which is a butcher shop from the 1800s.

1

Start drawing the St. Louis Cathedral by making three rectangles for the front.

2

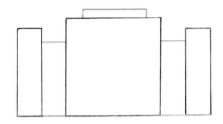

Add three more rectangles to the cathedral.

3

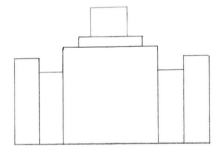

Draw one more rectangle on the top of the center section.

4

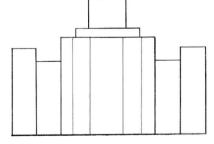

Draw four lines in the center rectangle to help shape the front of the cathedral.

5

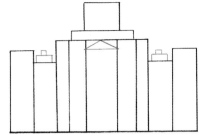

Add a triangle and four rectangles.

6

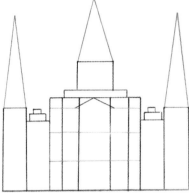

Draw lines across the building and add three triangles. Erase the extra line in the center.

7

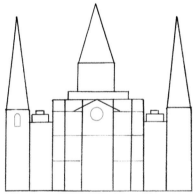

Add windows and a circle for the clock. Erase the line at the bottom of the building.

8

Finish the windows and add shading and detail to your building. Erase any extra smudges and you're done.

23

Mardi Gras

Mardi Gras celebrations have been held in Louisiana since the early 1700s. The first Mardi Gras parade was held in the 1830s. Mardi Gras, which means "Fat Tuesday" in French, is a time of fun and feasting before Lent, a 40-day period of prayer and sacrifice observed by certain Christians. During Mardi Gras, floats parade down St. Charles Avenue. People on the floats toss necklaces with purple, green, and gold beads to the crowd watching from the street. These colors signify justice, faith, and power. The jester, dressed in a bright costume with bells on his hat and collar, adds to the celebration. Jesters entertained kings and queens in the Middle Ages.

1

Draw a circle and three triangles. Add a small circle for the jester's nose.

2

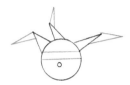

Add three more triangles for the jester's hat. Add two horizontal lines at the front of the circle.

3

Add three more triangles and three small circles to the hat. Draw in the shape of the face and of the mask.

4

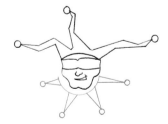

Erase extra lines. Add a half circle around the neck. Add four triangles with circles at the ends for the jester's collar.

5

Add eyes. Draw a rectangle for the jester's chest.

6

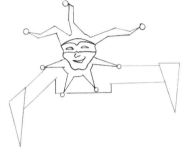

Add two rectangles for arms and two triangles for cuffs.

7

Add a rounded rectangle for the jester's body. Draw the jester's hands.

8

Add a pole under the figure using a thin rectangle. Add detail and shading.

The Alligator

In 1983, Louisiana chose the alligator as its official state reptile. American alligators live in many of Louisiana's waterways and lowland swamps. Alligators and their ancestors have existed on Earth for more than 230 million years. They usually grow to about 13 feet (4 m), although the largest alligator ever recorded was found in Louisiana. It measured 19 feet, 2 inches (6 m). Alligators can weigh up to 500 pounds (227 kg). Small alligators eat snails, insects, frogs, and small fish. Larger alligators eat turtles, snakes, birds, smaller alligators, and sometimes even deer and cattle. These powerful reptiles swallow their food whole!

1

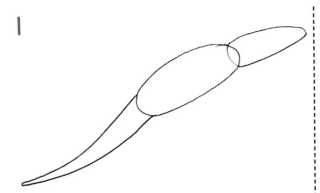

Begin by drawing two long ovals for the head and body of the alligator. Then add a long tail.

2

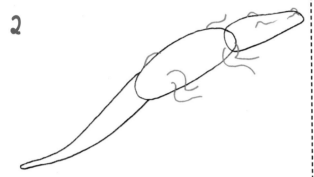

Draw the outlines of the legs and the lumps where the alligator's eyes and nostrils stick up. The eyes and nostrils stand on top of the alligator's head so it can hide underwater but can still see and smell prey.

3

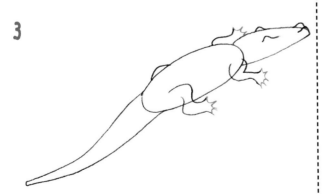

Draw webbed feet. These help the alligator swim fast.

4

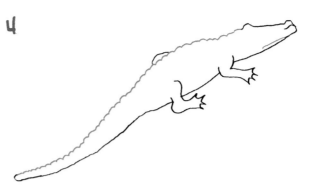

Redraw the alligator's back making it scaly and bumpy. Draw in the alligator's mouth. Erase any extra lines.

5

Add lines to give the alligator's skin a bumpy texture. Add the alligator's eye.

6

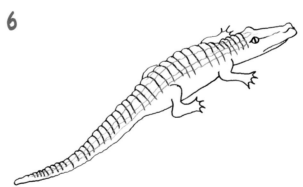

Add more lines to the back for the alligator's skin.

27

Louisiana's Capitol

Louisiana's capitol building is in Baton Rouge, the state's capital city. At 34 stories and 450 feet (137 m) high, it is the tallest capitol in the United States. It stands on a 27-acre (11-ha) plot of land. The capitol took only 14 months to build. It was completed in 1932. It took 2,500 freight cars to haul the marble and limestone used to build the capitol. In 1935, Louisiana governor Huey P. Long, who oversaw the building's construction, was assassinated in the capitol.

The steps leading up to the front of the building represent each state that existed at the time of its construction. Statues that represent law, science, philosophy, and art stand in the four corners of the building's tower.

1

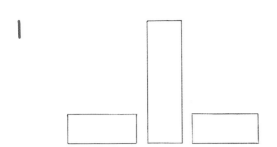

Start by drawing three large rectangles for the front of the building.

2

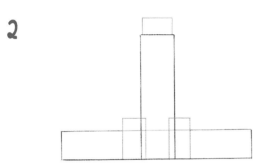

Add three more rectangles to the building. Draw an extra line as shown.

3

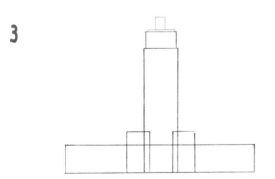

Add two more rectangles to the top of the center building.

4

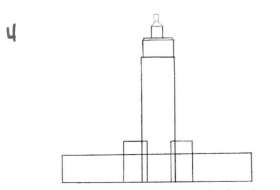

Draw a triangle and a rectangle for the top of the building.

5

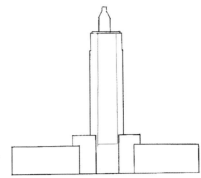

Erase extra lines and add a large rectangle to the center building.

6

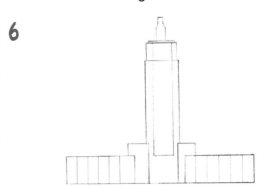

Draw five lines in each small rectangle at the sides of the building.

7

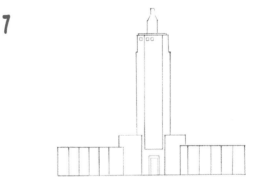

Add small squares for windows and rectangles for the door.

8

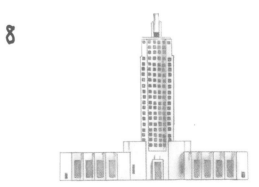

Finish the windows and add shading and detail to your building. Erase any extra smudges.

Louisiana State Facts

Statehood	April 30, 1812, 18th state
Area	49,651 square miles (128,596 sq km)
Population	4,372,000
Capital	Baton Rouge, population 215,900
Most Populated City	New Orleans, population 476,600
Industries	Chemical and petroleum products, paper products, food processing, tourism
Agriculture	Sugarcane, rice, dairy products, poultry
Tree	Bald cypress
Song	"Give Me Louisiana"
Nickname	The Pelican State
Motto	Union, Justice, & Confidence
Bird	Eastern brown pelican
Flower	Magnolia flower
Fossil	Petrified palmwood
Gemstone	Agate
Dog	Louisiana catahoula leopard dog
Crustacean	Crawfish
Reptile	Alligator
Insect	Honeybee
Instrument	Diatonic "Cajun" accordion

Glossary

adopted (uh-DOPT-ed) To have accepted or approved something.

ancestry (AN-ses-tree) Having to do with a person's relatives who lived long ago.

assassinated (uh-SA-sin-ayt-ed) To have murdered an important or famous person.

bayous (BY-yooz) Bodies of slow-moving water.

botanist (BAH-tun-est) A person who studies flowers.

carnival (KAR-nuh-vuhl) A fair with games and rides.

celebrations (seh-luh-BRAY-shunz) Observances of special times, with activities.

Civil War (SIH-vul WOR) The war fought between the northern and southern states of America from 1861 to 1865.

confidence (KON-fih-dents) A firm belief in oneself and one's abilities.

culture (KUL-chur) The beliefs, customs, art, and religions of a group of people.

descendants (dih-SEN-dents) People born of a certain family or group.

Dixieland (DIK-see-land) Jazz music played by a small band.

entertained (en-ter-TAYND) To have kept someone interested or amused.

herbal remedy (ER-buhl REH-meh-dee) Medicine made from plants.

industries (IN-dus-treez) Systems of work, or labor.

levees (LEH-veez) Raised riverbanks used to stop a river from overflowing.

philosophy (fuh-LAH-suh-fee) The study of the basic nature of reality and life.

plantation (plan-TAY-shun) A very large farm where crops are grown.

reservoir (REH-zuh-vwahr) A stored body of water.

sacrifice (SA-krih-fys) To give up something for an ideal or a belief.

union (YOON-yun) The bringing together of two or more things.

Union (YOON-yun) The northern states that stayed loyal to the federal government during the Civil War.

Index

Web Sites

To learn more about Louisiana, check out this Web site:
www.state.la.us